MW01060232

All About California

100+ Amazing Facts with Color Pictures

By Bandana Ojha

All rights reserved. This book or any portion thereof may not be reproduced or used in any manner without the express written permission of the author.

Copyright © 2021 By the author.

Introduction

Filled with up-to-date information, fascinating & fun facts this book " All About California: 100+ Interesting & Amazing Facts that Everyone Should Know" is the best book for kids to find out more about the Golden State. This book would satisfy the children's curiosity and help them to understand why California is special—and what makes it different from other States. This book gives a story, history & explores the interesting and amazing fun facts about California. It's a fun and fascinating way for young readers to find out more California state facts and all bits of information that can touch the kid's inquisitive mind. This is a great chance for every kid to expand their knowledge about California and impress family and friends with all the discovered and never known before facts.

1. California became an official state of the United States on Monday, September 9, 1850.

2. The name California comes from a 16th-century Spanish novel written by a Spanish author named Garcia Ordonez de Montalvo. that describes a mythical paradise called California.

3. California is the third largest state, following Alaska and Texas. It is 1,040 miles long, and 560 miles wide.

4. California has almost 39 million residents, more than Canada and roughly 1/8 of U.S. population.

5. California is bordered by the Pacific Ocean in the west, Oregon in the north, Nevada and Arizona in the east, and Mexico in the south.

6. The Californian economy is the largest economy in the U.S.

7. California was the first state in the USA to reach 1 trillion dollars GDP.

8. If California was its own country, it would have the 6th largest economy in the world.

9. 13. State Abbreviation of California is "CA".

10. People of California are called Californians.

11. The General Sherman tree is found in Sequoia National Park California and is believed to be the world's largest tree by volume.

12. World's first McDonald's restaurant was opened in 1940, by brothers Richard and Maurice McDonald in San Bernardino, California.

13. The highest and lowest points in mainland U.S. are both in California. Mount Whitney stands at 14,495 feet, and only 76 miles away is Death Valley which is 282 feet below sea level.

14. Los Angeles is the largest city in California.

15. Capital of California is "Sacramento".

16. The official State flag is "Flag of California'.

17. The official state flag also called the Bear Flag. It was first used on June 14, 1846, but officially adopted in 1911.

18. State flag was designed by William Todd, nephew of Mary Todd Lincoln.

19. The official state bird is California valley quail.

20. The State grain is Rice.

21. The State fruit is Avocado.

22. The official state mammal is Grizzly bear.

23. The official State Marine Mammal is Gray whale.

24. The official state reptile is Desert tortoise.

25. The official state fish is Golden trout.

26. The state marine fish is Garibaldi.

27. The state insect is California dogface butterfly.

28. The State Flower is California Poppy.

29. The State tree is Redwood tree.

30. The State Grass is Purple Needlegrass.

31. The State Fossil Smilodon californicus.

32. The State Rock is Serpentinite.

33. The State soil is San Joaquin.

34. The State nick name is "The Golden State".

35. The state nickname came to be in 1968, representing the discovery of gold in 1848 and the fields of golden poppies seen each spring.

36. The State song is "I Love You, California" written by F.B. Silverwood, a Los Angeles merchant.

37. The State Motto is "Eureka "(I have found it).

38. The official state colors are Blue and Gold.

39. The State Mineral is Gold.

40. The state Gemstone is Benitoite.

40. The State dance is west coast swing.

41. The State folk dance is Square Dance.

42. 44. The State nuts are Almond, Walnut, Pistachio and Pecan.

43. Augustynolophus morrisi became California's official state dinosaur in 2017.

44. The State sport is Surfing.

45. The state fabric is Denim.

46. Los Angeles, San Diego and San Jose of California are all in top ten largest U. S. cities.

47. Richard Milhous Nixon was born in Yorba Linda, CA on January 9, 1913. He was the 37th US President, serving from 1969 to 1974.

48. Death Valley is also the hottest and driest place in the country. Summer temperatures often reach over 115 degrees.

49. There was a massive gold rush in the 1800s, and that's how it became the Golden State

50. California is home to the "Avocado Capital of the World." Every year, Fallbrook holds an avocado festival to celebrate.

51. California is the only state that's hosted both the Summer and Winter Olympics.

52. California is a multicultural state with many ethnic groups and cultures. That's also what makes the state so diverse and rich.

53. 1/4 of the Californian population are born outside the U.S

54. Several Native American groups lived in California — Yuma, Maidu, Pomo, Hupa and Paiute tribes live in California.

55. Hyperion, a coastal redwood in Redwood National Park, California is the tallest living tree, at 379.1 feet.

56. San Bernardino County, California is the largest county in the U.S.

57. Alpine County is the eighth smallest of California's 58 counties. It has no high school, ATMs, dentists, banks, or traffic lights.

58. The Gold Rush was the largest mass migration in United States history.

59. California is known for its vast production of fruit and vegetables. It yields most of the country's peaches, plums, artichokes, and broccoli.

60. Almonds are the biggest export of California.

61. The original Disneyland theme park was built in Anaheim, California in 1955. It is the only theme park designed and built under the management of Walt Disney.

62. California's economy is larger than the economies of many countries of the world.

63. Computing and technology, agriculture, movie production and tourism are the major Industries of California.

64. With nine national parks, California is home to the most national parks in the entire United States.

65. It is home to a wide variety of tourist attractions – San Francisco, Disneyworld, San Diego Zoo, Golden Gate Bridge, Lake Tahoe, Yosemite, Hollywood, Beverly Hills and many more.

66. California is one of the largest, most economically successful, and is one of the most popular places to visit in the world.

67. There are more than 300,000 tons of grapes grown in California annually.

68. Due to its Mediterranean climate, California can produce over 17 million gallons of wine each year.

69. Fresno, California is known as the Raisin Capital of the World.

70. California is the birthplace of Fortune Cookie, Apple computer, theme park (Disneyland), Frisbee, the Barbie dolls, skateboards, and video arcade games.

71. The state has 482 incorporated cities and towns, of which 460 are cities and 22 are towns.

72. California also known as The Land of Milk and Honey, The El Dorado State and The Grape State

73. Castroville, California known for its artichoke crop and for the annual Castroville Artichoke Festival, leading to its nickname as the "Artichoke Center of the World".

74. 72. Levi Strauss, a 44-year-old German immigrant, invented the first blue jeans in San Francisco on May 20, 1873.

75. Californians experienced a unique weather phenomenon in 1955 when the snowfall was green with a phosphorescent effect. Residents who decided to try the language of its cereals soon died and the people who took the snow in their hands got rashes and intense itching.

76. San Francisco's cable cars are the only National Historical Monument that can move. The cables that pull the cars run at a constant speed of 9.5 MPH.

77. San Francisco Bay is considered the world's largest landlocked harbor. It's 60 miles long and three to 12 miles wide.

78. The Hollywood Bowl is the world's largest outdoor amphitheater.

79. Located in Sacramento, the California State Railroad Museum is the largest museum of its kind in North America.

80. In 1925 a giant sequoia located in California's Kings Canyon National Park was named the nation's national Christmas tree. The tree is over 300 feet in height.

81. California is in the Pacific Time Zone and observes Daylight Savings Time.

82. It is estimated there are approximately 500,000 detectable seismic tremors in California annually.

83. The first motion picture theater opened in Los Angeles on April 2, 1902.

84. More movies have been filmed in California than any other state in US

85.California grows over 90 percent of the broccoli that's produced in the United States.

86. More turkeys are raised in California than in any other state in the United States.

87. California is home to the most famous technology companies in the world – so much so that they have named the area where they are located 'Silicon Valley'

88. California's constitution is one of the longest collections of laws in the world.

89. The California state seal was created when the state was first formed in 1849. The idea came from Caleb Lyon, a clerk of the California Constitutional Convention, but the design of the California state seal was done by Major R. S. Garnett of the United States Army.

90. The total number of California counties are 58.

91.Thirty-one Stars in State seal represents number of states after California was admitted.

92. Some California plants live a long time. The eastern Sierras' Bristlecone pines are 4,600 years old, but a Mojave Desert creosote bush is among the world's oldest living things at 43,000 years

93. California is the most populous state in United States.

94. In the midpoint of California, there is a palm tree and a pine tree planted next to each other to signify the meeting point of Northern and Southern California

95. Walt Disney Concert Hall is the largest performing arts centers in the United States.

96. The United Nations Charter was drafted and ratified in San Francisco in 1945.

97 The popular burger chain In-N-Out first opened in California which was California's first drive through burger stand in 1948. No stores were opened outside California until 1992.

98. California contains the most diverse environment in the world It varies from hot desert to subarctic depending on latitude and elevation.

99. Bosco Ramos was a dog elected honorary mayor of the unincorporated community of Sunol, California

100. The fortune cookie was inspired by the Japanese fortune tradition o-mikuji and invented in California

101. The Mojave Desert, at more than 25,000 square miles (65,000 square km), occupies one-sixth of the land area of California.

102. Furnace Creek in Death Valley is where the hottest temperature on Earth was recorded 134.1 degrees Fahrenheit (on July 10, 1913).

103. Mount Whitney in California is the highest point in the U.S., outside of Alaska.

104. Clear Lake is the largest natural lake wholly within the state. It has a surface area of 68 square miles.

105. Death Valley (at 3.4 million acres) in California is the largest U.S. National Park outside of Alaska.

106. When Golden Gate Bridge was built, it spanned 4,200 feet and staked its claim as the longest suspension bridge in the world. and it held this record until 1964. That's over 25 years. In 1964, it was finally surpassed by the Verrazano Bridge in New York City.

Please check this out:

Our other best-selling books for kids are-

Know about **Sharks**: 100 Amazing Fun Facts with Pictures

Know About **Whales**:100+ Amazing & Interesting Fun Facts with Pictures: " Never known Before "- Whales facts

Know About **Dinosaurs**: 100 Amazing & Interesting Fun Facts with Pictures

Know About **Kangaroos**: Amazing & Interesting Facts with Pictures

Know About **Penguins**: 100+ Amazing Penguin Facts with Pictures

Know About **Dolphins** :100 Amazing Dolphin Facts with Pictures

Know About **Elephant** :100 Amazing Dolphin Facts with Pictures

All About **New York**: 100+ Amazing Facts with Pictures

All About **New Jersey**: 100+ Amazing Facts with Pictures

All About **Massachusetts**: 100+ Amazing Facts with Pictures

All About **Florida**: 100+ Amazing Facts with Pictures

All About **California**: 100+ Amazing Facts with Pictures

All About **Arizona**: 100+ Amazing Facts with Pictures

All About **Texas**: 100+ Amazing Facts with Pictures

All About **Minnesota**: 100+ Amazing Facts with Pictures

All About **New Mexico**: 100+ Amazing Facts with Pictures

All About **Italy**: 100+ Amazing Facts with Pictures

All About **France**: 100+ Amazing Facts with Pictures

All About **Japan:** 100 Amazing & Interesting Fun Facts

100 Amazing **Quiz Q & A About Penguin**: Never Known Before Penguin Facts

Most Popular **Animal Quiz** book for Kids: 100 amazing animal facts

Quiz Book for Kids: Science, History, Geography, Biology, Computer & Information Technology

English **Grammar** for Kids: Most Easy Way to learn English Grammar

Solar System & Space Science- Quiz for Kids: What You Know About Solar System

English **Grammar Practice** Book for elementary kids: 1000+ Practice Questions with Answers

A to Z of **English Tense**

My First **Fruits**

Made in the USA
Columbia, SC
22 May 2021

38275424R00026